DEVOTIONS
FOR
EARLY TEENS

Volume Two

by

RUTH I. JOHNSON

Assistant editor of "Young Ambassador"

JUNIOR HIGH LEVEL

MOODY PRESS
CHICAGO

Printed in the United States of America

FOREWORD

This second volume of devotions for teens contains 60 messages. These deal with practical and enduring truths; consequently, each message will be turned to many times for instruction and spiritual encouragement.

Maximum benefit will be derived from the devotional helps when the Bible portions are read prayerfully and the verses quoted are committed to memory.

Ruth Johnson is currently assistant editor of *Young Ambassador,* our monthly Gospel paper for youth. She is also director of the Ambassador Youth Choir, heard each Saturday over the special international network of the Back to the Bible Broadcast.

—John I. Paton
Literature Editor

CONTENTS

1

GRETA TENSHUN
(Get attention)

A Bible Tip
I Timothy 4:12-16; 5:1,2

A Memory Tip
"Talk no more so exceeding proudly; let not arrogancy come out of your mouth: for the Lord is a God of knowledge, and by him actions are weighed" (I Sam. 2:3).

A Timely Tip
The six teen-agers boarded the city bus, and paid their fare, then stood near the entrance. They had made it a special point to get on first, leaving a crippled man and an elderly woman to wait.

"Step to the rear, please," called the bus driver, for there were still quite a number of people who had not been able to get any farther than the doorway. One of the boys called back in a loud, mocking voice, "Step to the rear, please; that's what the man said." All six of the teens laughed noisily, and the boy must have felt rewarded for this loud "attention getter."

For the next 15 or 20 minutes as the bus traveled through the city, the teens talked about everything from hot rods to hot dogs, and loud enough so that everyone on the bus had to listen to their conversation. They laughed boisterously at a little old man who fumbled for his change and nervously dropped it to the floor. They sang parts of their school song and referred to their teachers as "Old man so and so" and "Old lady so and so."

If they were after attention, they got it, but not the kind they should have sought.

Watching all this, I couldn't help but wish that these teens knew the Lord. And then, as they got off the bus, I saw something that surprised me — they were carrying their Bibles along with their other books! *If they were Christians, they surely hadn't convinced anyone that day.*

We must be careful so that even our daily actions witness for the Lord.

A Final Tip
Speech and actions may betray,
That your life has gone astray.

2

MORT, AL, LEE WOONDID
(Mortally wounded)

I John 5:1-5

A Bible Tip

A Memory Tip

"Ye are of God, little children, and have overcome them: because greater is he that is in you, than he that is in the world" (I John 4:4).

A Timely Tip

The Woondid brothers were three fellows that everyone knew they had to watch out for. And all three of them were the same. They were so touchy that almost everything hurt them.

If someone had a secret and didn't let them in on it, they became very offended. If they heard about a party, and learned that they weren't to be invited, they pouted. If someone was shown some favor, and they didn't get a favor shown to them, they were hurt. They were well named Mort, Al, Lee Woondid — mortally wounded.

The more they were neglected, the worse it seemed to get; and the worse it got, the more people seemed to neglect them. In fact, people rarely wanted to include them in any of the activities because of their attitudes.

Pouty, chip-on-the-shoulder, easily hurt Christians are not too pleasant to be with. They spoil everything for everyone else; and more than that, their actions must certainly displease the Saviour.

If you are one of these easily wounded Christians, admit it to God as sin, and ask Him to help you to overcome it. Then thank Him for the victory in your life.

"But, I'm almost sure to do it again," you say. "What if I fail?"

Then start again. Ask the Lord for forgiveness, thank Him for the victory in your life and go on. So you fail a third time and a fourth? — start over again! Each time you come to Him in a humble, repentant spirit, you will find it easier to overcome this sin.

A Final Tip

Wounded easily, hurt inside?
Get the vict'ry over pride.

3

GROVER N. TELL

(Go over and tell)

A Bible Tip

John 1:35-42

A Memory Tip

"Also I heard the voice of the Lord, saying, Whom shall I send, and who will go for us? Then said I, Here am I; send me" (Isa. 6:8).

A Timely Tip

The service in the church was coming to a close and the invitation song was being sung. A young boy came down the aisle indicating his desire to accept Christ as his Saviour. As he came to the front, the minister talked with him for a moment and then the deacons took him into a small prayer room just off the main sanctuary.

As they opened the door, the young boy turned and ran out of the room.

"Just as I thought," said one of the old deacons, "that boy didn't mean business at all. He ran out just the minute we were going to talk with him."

But before any of the other deacons had time to agree, the door flew open and in walked the young lad. With him was a tall, slender man.

"I went to get my father," said the boy. "If Jesus can do what the minister said, then I know my dad wants Him, too."

Of course, the old deacon was shocked and had to confess that he had been wrong in his criticism.

One day a young man by the name of Andrew heard John the Baptist introducing the Lord Jesus. Andrew was so struck by what he heard, that he went in search of his brother, Peter.

"Come with me," he called to his brother. "Come and see. We have found the Messiah."

Who have you told about Jesus? When you first heard about Him, did you run out and find someone else to be sure that he would hear about Him, too?

When we look back at what some of these others have done, we are put to shame at the little we do.

A Final Tip

Someone gave the truth to you,
So it's the least that you can do.

4

OLIVE T. ENHERET
(Alive to inherit)

A Bible Tip
I Corinthians 6:9-12

A Memory Tip

"Likewise reckon ye also yourselves to be dead indeed unto sin, but alive unto God through Jesus Christ our Lord" (Rom. 6:11).

A Timely Tip

In a large city newspaper recently there was an item that caught the attention of almost all the readers. It told of an estate which was to go to a certain person. But when the attorneys went to locate this person, they found that he had just died. The estate could not go to him, for a dead person cannot inherit an estate, or anything else.

This is not only true in the physical, but it is also true in the spirtual. There is a large estate in Heaven. In fact, when Jesus was about to leave his disciples, he told them about the estate. He called it a mansion.

But people who are dead — dead in trespasses and sin — cannot inherit the kingdom of God.

Another time Jesus was talking to a ruler. He said, "Nicodemus, Ye must be born again." In other words, Jesus was telling him that he must have life; life in Christ Jesus before he could inherit the kingdom of God. Neither can we inherit it if we are dead.

Now, what if the law did permit a dead man to inherit an estate? What if the newspapermen and the attorneys had agreed that it belonged to the dead man. Then what? What could he have done with it? The property would have stood unused and soon become run down and useless. He could not have cared for it or controlled it, for he was dead.

In order to enjoy something you must have life; you must be living. So, in order to enjoy the things of the Lord, you must be living, you must be born again, you must have eternal life through Jesus Christ, God's Son. Do you have this life, or must it be said of you that you are dead — dead in trespasses and sin?

A Final Tip

If you're dead, you can't inherit,
There must be life if you're going to share it.

5

WADE N. HYMN
(Wait on Him)

A Bible Tip

Psalm 25:1-14

A Memory Tip

"The Lord is good unto them that wait for him, to the soul that seeketh him. It is good that a man should both hope and quietly wait for the salvation of the Lord" (Lam. 3:25, 26).

A Timely Tip

There were two ships that were stranded. As the captains of the ships communicated with one another, they agreed that they would not be able to move until the high tide came in.

However, one of the captains was very impatient. He had gone through this before, and he knew that it could be a long wait. And this he did not enjoy. Suddenly he had an idea. He told the captain of the other ship about it, but this captain was unimpressed.

"I'll do it anyway," he said to himself, and then set to work with his plan.

He sent word to have one hundred horses brought near the place where his ship was. They were to pull him out.

It was no small task getting the one hundred horses, but the captain had ordered it, so arrangements were made. Word got around quickly and soon a large crowd had come to see the one hundred horses pull the ship.

The horses pulled and pulled. But rather than getting the ship out, the people saw the vessel begin to break and soon it was broken into pieces. Yes, the horses pulled all right, but their strength pulled the ship to bits.

The other captain sat and waited for the high tide, and in a few days he was able to return safe and sound to the harbor.

Sometimes we get so impatient that we want to do things our way and in our time. We should wait for God's direction, for His way is always the best way. One hundred horses cannot be better than God's strong hand. Let us learn to wait for Him in everything we do.

A Final Tip

A hundred horses cannot do,
What God's strong arm has planned for you.

6

WANDA YETHREE
(One yet three)

A Bible Tip
John 16:7-15

A Memory Tip

"The grace of the Lord Jesus Christ, and the love of God, and the communion of the Holy Ghost,, be with you all" (II Cor. 13:14).

A Timely Tip

Sometimes young people feel it is difficult to understand the teaching concerning the Trinity. They do not know how God, the Father; God, the Son; and God, the Holy Spirit can be three and still be one. Young people wonder if they should pray to God, the Father, or to the Son, or to the Holy Spirit.

To help us understand the Trinity a little better, let us take a look at the American flag. What are its colors? Red, white, and blue. In fact, it is sometimes called the "Red, White, and Blue."

When you were in elementary school, no doubt your

18

teacher asked you to salute the flag. When she did this, did you say, "Which one? the red, the white, or the blue?" Of course not. When the teacher asked you to salute the flag, you saluted the flag — all three colors.

Yes, it contains three colors, but it is still only one flag.

The same is true with regards to God, Father, Son, and Holy Spirit. One God, yet three in one.

The egg is also used to clarify this truth. It is one egg, but it is also a yolk, a white, and a shell.

A river contains many drops of water, but it becomes one body; a watch has many parts, but we do not speak of the individual parts, but rather the watch itself.

God, the Father; God, the Son; and God, the Holy Spirit — three — yet one!

And one of the great truths about it all is that this God dwells within us. Our bodies become His home. It is as though He is the tenant and we the landlord. Should we not be more careful then, how we live?

A Final Tip
God, the Father, and the Son,
And the Spirit all are one.

19

7

BURT N. ANIMUL
(Bird and animal)

A Bible Tip

Ephesians 2:1-13

A Memory Tip

"Therefore if any man be in Christ, he is a new creature: old things are passed away; behold, all things are become new" (II Cor. 5:17).

Did you ever try to have a talking session with birds or animals? Who did all the talking? You! Did they even one time answer back in your language? Of course not! True, certain birds can be trained to say certain words and phrases, but they can never carry on an intelligent conversation with you. Well, why not? Because they aren't human. And it will always be impossible for them to really communicate with you unless human powers and a human nature could be put in them. In their present condition birds and animals cannot intelligently communicate with man.

Neither can the fellow or girl who has not been made a new creature in Christ Jesus have any real communion with God. If we want to be on speaking terms with Him, we must first be changed. We must become children of God. There is only one way for this to be done — it must be done on God's terms.

If you will confess you are a sinner and trust in Christ to save you, you will be given a new nature. The Bible says that you will be made a new creation.

A dog can live in a home with human beings for many years, but that does not make him a human being. In the same way a person can attend church for many years, but that does not make him a Christian. He must be made a new creature in Christ Jesus; not just his surroundings changed, but a complete heart change. This will make it possible for him to fellowship with God.

Yes, old things must pass away and all things must become new.

A Final Tip
Speaking terms can be arranged,
Only when your heart is changed.

8

JOY N. SHARIN
(Joy in sharing)

A Bible Tip
Ecclesiastes 5:13-20

A Memory Tip

"Thus saith the Lord, Let not the wise man glory in his wisdom, neither let the mighty man glory in his might, let not the rich man glory in his riches: But let him that glorieth in this, that he understandeth and knoweth me . . ." (Jer. 9:23, 24).

A Timely Tip

When a London businessman first opened his business, he wrote down four rules for his life, and these he practiced for the next fifty years. His slogan was this: "If I become rich, let me not be too joyful in having, too solicitous in keeping, too anxious in increasing, or too sorrowful in losing."

In everyday teen-age language, this simply means, that if God should allow you to make good money, that you will not become so thrilled with making or having the money that you will forget God; also, that you will not be so intent on keeping it, or increasing it, that if you should lose it, you will forget God.

The Lord honored this man and gave him riches, because He knew that He could trust him with it. For fifty years the man enjoyed wealth, but he used it for the glory of God.

I wonder, could God trust you and me with a great deal of wealth? Would we become too selfish if He showered these things on us?

It might be well for us to take this motto, "If God gives me wealth, may I not be too joyful in having, too solicitous in keeping, too anxious in increasing, nor too sorrowful in losing."

This must be our attitude in everything that God gives us: Money, friends, health, home, and all.

If God entrusted you with some of these, could this honestly be your motto?

A Final Tip

If He should give, if He should take,
I know He never will forsake.

9

CON VIC SHUNS
(Convictions)

A Bible Tip
I John 2:3-7

A Memory Tip

"For I know whom I have believed, and am persuaded that he is able to keep that which I have committed unto him against that day. That good thing which was committed unto thee keep by the Holy Ghost which dwelleth in us" (II Tim. 1:12, 14).

A Timely Tip

Do you have any convictions? Real honest to goodness convictions? For example, what is your attitude toward your mother and father? toward the Lord? toward the Bible? toward truth? toward sin? What are your convictions on these things? What do you believe?

Paul said, "I know whom I have believed, and am persuaded that he is able to keep that which I have committed unto him against that day." What do you have to say on the subject? If you had to come right out and tell what you believed, what would you say?

Do the kids in school know what you stand for, or are they pretty sure they can "talk you out" of almost anything?

When the school prom question comes up, where do you stand? When the dance after the big game is brought up, where do you stand? When the school band starts playing swing and jazz, where do you stand? When the gym class becomes a dancing instruction hour, where do you stand? When your science teacher says men and monkeys came from the same ancestry, where do you stand? When he says the Bible is no longer an accepted book, where do you stand?

Do you have any convictions at all? If so, what are they? Do the students and teachers alike know how you feel? Do they know that your salvation is real to you and not just something that you accepted because it was handed down from your family? Do they know that you believe it and that you just weren't talked into it at a weak moment?

What really are your convictions? Where do you stand?

A Final Tip
Your convictions may demand,
That you take a better stand.

10

HARTLEY BY LENGTH
(Hardly by length)

A Bible Tip

Luke 18:10-14

A Memory Tip

"Woe unto you, scribes and Pharisees, hypocrites! for ye devour widows' houses, and for a pretence make long prayer: therefore ye shall receive the greater damnation" (Matt. 23:14).

A Timely Tip

Have you ever been to a concert? After the musician is through playing, the applause from the audience is tremendous. Why do they applaud? Because he played such a long number? Of course not, but because he played so well. Quantity has very little to do with it. It's quality that counts.

Some people get the feeling that prayer goes by quantity. If they pray long prayers in public, remembering every missionary, every need, and every situation, they feel they have impressed God — and God's people too.

26

A little boy asked his father one day, "Dad, does God know everything?"

"Why, yes, son," said the father. "God is all knowing."

"Are you sure?" asked the little boy.

"I'm absolutely sure," replied the father. "Why do you ask?"

"Because when some people pray, they take so long telling God everything I just thought maybe God wasn't posted."

Long prayers, especially in the privacy of our personal devotions, are not to be discouraged. But when we pray, we should talk with God — not give Him a discourse, nor a list of wants and wishes — but simply take some time to fellowship with Him. How He must miss our genuine everyday fellowship!

Sometimes you call a friend on the telephone, not because you have a request to make, but simply because you want to talk with him. And when you do this, you don't stop and check the clock to be sure you talk a certain length of time, or check the dictionary to see that you use the right words. You simply enjoy each other.

The next time you pause to pray, don't do it by the clock, do it by your heart.

A Final Tip

A two-way conversation,
Can be an inspiration.

27

11

OLIVE ASILIK
(I'll live as I like)

A Bible Tip

II Timothy 3:1-5

A Memory Tip

"Be not thou therefore ashamed of the testimony of our Lord..." (II Tim. 1:8).

A Timely Tip

Olive had accepted the Lord Jesus as her personal Saviour when she was eleven years old, but lately it seemed that church was not as important as "the gang."

Only at her father's insistence had she finally invited the gang to attend the special meetings at the church, but she had to admit that she was embarrassed when she did it, and surprised when they agreed to go.

When the invitation was given at the close of the service, Olive was under conviction. She remembered when she had really lived for the Lord, and put Him first in her life. Now, it seemed that the gang came first. She bowed her head reverently and asked the Lord to forgive her. Then she began praying for the members of the gang to accept Christ. For a moment it looked as though Bill would take the step; he moved about nervously, putting his hands in his pockets and jingling the change until he realized he was making a noise. The other kids seemed to be stirred by the message too, but none of them made a decision for Christ.

After the benediction, everyone piled in Bill's car and drove to a nearby town for something to eat. All during the drive they joked and laughed hilariously, and Olive decided that they were trying to cover up their true feelings.

And then it happened. She could faintly remember hearing the train whistle, but that was all. Now in the hospital she asked, "The other kids ... How are the other kids?" The deep silence gave her the answer. They had lost their lives, and none of them knew the Saviour.

Yes, she had invited them to church, but she hadn't really been burdened for them. She had compromised; she could see that now. From now on she would no longer live as she liked, but rather in a way that she could lead others to the Saviour.

A Final Tip

My life is really not my own,
And witnessing I won't postpone.

12

GROVER GRASS
(Grow over grass)

A Bible Tip
Ezra 9:5-8

A Memory Tip

"And in the morning, rising up a great while before day, he went out, and departed into a solitary place and there prayed" (Mark 1:35).

A Timely Tip

Many years ago when the missionaries working in the dark land of Africa were first beginning to produce a few converts, the Christian natives were taught and encouraged to have a "quiet time" with God.

Since they did not have rooms or other places where they could go to have their private devotions, the natives got into the habit of going out into the jungle. Each person would pick a certain spot in the thicket where he would go every day to pray to his newly found Saviour.

After the converts increased and more of them

learned to have a quiet time with the Lord, quite a number of the jungle places were distinctly marked. All over the jungle could be found small spots where the grass was worn off.

Whenever it was noticed that one of the places seemed to be growing grass again, the other Christians would go to the person whose spot was not used as often as it had been, and say, "Brother, the grass is growing on your path."

Fortunately, or perhaps unfortunately, we do not have these places today. If our friends knew how much time we spent in prayer, would we be so ashamed that we would again make it a regular habit? Remember, even though our friends may not know, God knows. And our spiritual lives show it.

Christian young person, is the grass growing on your path? Or is your "daily kneeling" taking care of it? Take a look at your place of prayer. Does it show signs of constant use? Or could your friends say, "The grass is growing on your path."

A Final Tip

When the grass is showing thickness,
Check yourself for spiritual sickness.

13

DREW M. AWAY
(Drew them away)

A Bible Tip

James 1:13-18

A Memory Tip

"Thine own mouth condemneth thee, and not I; yea, thine own lips testify against thee" (Job 15:6).

A Timely Tip

Jim had been praying for two of his school friends for some time. At his father's suggestion, he had saved all his earnings from his paper route in order to pay the way for both his friends to go with him to Bible camp. "Maybe they will come to know Christ as their Saviour there," said Jim.

It was made a matter of family prayer, and finally the day for leaving for camp arrived. Jim and his buddies were the first on the bus. There was expectancy in the air, and Jim had the feeling that everything was going just right.

But at camp Jim decided to go all out for fun. "Let's

switch the salt with the sugar in the dining hall," suggested Jim to his two friends. The boys went for it in a big way.

"Let's unscrew a fuse and the lights will go out during the service," suggested one of the boys, and Jim went along with that.

"Let's let some air out of the tires of the speaker's car," suggested the third boy, "and he will get stuck here all night."

The ideas became bigger and worse each time. By the end of the week, Jim tried to talk with the boys about accepting Christ as their Saviour. But they laughed at him and told him he in no way was different from them.

Sometimes we don't realize that the little pranks we pull help determine an eternal destiny for someone — the wrong way.

The Word of God says, "Do all to the glory of God." What you did today, or what you will be doing today — is it for His glory?

A Final Tip

Things you think are cute or clever,
Don't win souls to Christ; no, never.

14

HOWIE FINRENS
(How we find friends)

A Bible Tip

Ephesians 3: 14-21

A Memory Tip

"But what things were gain to me, those I counted loss for Christ. Yea doubtless, and I count all things but loss for the excellency of the knowledge of Christ Jesus my Lord..." (Phil. 3:7,8).

A Timely Tip

"The reason she has so many friends is that she is cute!" 'I know why he is on the top of the list; he's got money!" "His dad's a big shot, that's why everyone likes him." "She's got scads of clothes, that's why people take to her."

These are some of the statements that are made by teen-agers today. But this is idle talk, not facts. Friendship is not based on beauty, riches, position, nor clothes. Do you want to know how to make friends? The Bible tells you how. Be friendly! It's just that simple.

Friendliness includes respect, sincerity, convictions, genuineness, and things that come from the depth of the heart. If you want more friends, learn to develop some of your inner traits, rather than some of your present outer traits.

To begin with, you should forget the "I" in your life. Selfishness, selfish thoughts, and self-centeredness are the farthest things from friendliness. Some people are always talking about themselves. Give your thoughts to the needs of others. Don't make cutting remarks about them. Make kind remarks about them. If you can't say something kind, better that you say nothing.

Be dependable; be friendly; be pleasant, and by all means, be sincere. Make Christianity so attractive that others will want the Christ who lives in you. That doesn't mean that you will sit around in a corner and read your Bible so that everyone can see it. But it does mean that your life, your love, your interest, and your sincerity will all show for Christ. Then you will find that you will be helpful, interested, and genuine. You will be you, and Christ will shine through your life.

A Final Tip

If you're friendly and sincere,
Then your witness will be clear.

15

WILLIE OBEYEM
(Will he obey them)

A Bible Tip

Proverbs 3:1-12

A Memory Tip

"Obey them that have the rule over you, and submit yourselves: for they watch for your souls, as they that must give account, that they may do it with joy, and not with grief: for that is unprofitable for you" (Heb. 13:17).

A Timely Tip

Anyone who knows his Bible at all, or who has been in church or Sunday school for any length of time, knows that the Bible says, "Children, obey your parents in the Lord: for this is right. Honour thy father and mother; which is the first commandment with promise; That it may be well with thee, and thou mayest live long on the earth."

But knowing it and doing it can be two entirely different things. And often this brings on a family clash.

Dad says, "No"; Junior says, "Please." Mother says, "I should say not," and Sally says, "Why not?"

Many teen-agers think their parents are old-fashioned. Is this because they have not kept up with modern conveniences for the day? No, most present-day homes have those. Then where do we get the idea they are old-fashioned? There are plenty of other things that are old-fashioned — things that we have been doing for years, eating our meals, going to bed, taking a bath, and scores of other things — so that can't be it.

Is it just that we are not quite open-minded enough, that we hate to admit that they are still the boss, that they know just a tiny bit more than we do? Maybe the Bible knows what it is talking about when it says, "Children, obey your parents . . . for this is right."

Maybe the old-fashioned parents that you have in your house, also believe in the old-fashioned Gospel. If they do, thank the Lord for it and try your very best to live the way you ought to, pleasing to them, but more than that — pleasing to the Lord. You may not always agree with them, but you are to obey them in the Lord. Remember, they've had time to gain a little more knowledge, and maybe — just maybe, they might be right most of the time.

A Final Tip
Because of love and God's command,
I will obey and understand.

16

N. GLEE ECKT
(Neglect)

A Bible Tip

John 14:7-12

A Memory Tip

"I must work the words of him that sent me, while it is day: the night cometh, when no man can work" (John 9:4).

A Timely Tip

Sometimes we read in the newspaper that a certain businessman has been arrested for taking money from his company, completely ruining himself and the business. But a man does not necessarily have to commit robbery to ruin himself; all he needs to do is neglect his business. In just no time, his business will be run down.

A man lying on a bed of sickness, dangerously ill, does not need to take poison in order to die; all he needs to do is to neglect to take the right medicine, and his life will waste away.

A man riding on a rough sea in a small boat does not need to jump overboard to drown himself; he needs only to neglect to use the oar at the proper time and both he and his boat will be in serious trouble.

God's Word warns us about neglect. It tells us that we should not neglect so great a salvation. We do not need to be drunkards, murderers, or robbers in order to be doomed for Hell. Those who neglect this great salvation will be just as doomed as the robber, the murderer, or the drunkard.

God has provided the Way — the Lord Jesus. Should we neglect Him?

God has also given the Christian His Word. He has provided a way to read it, to hear it, and to meditate on it. Do you neglect to take advantage of this?

We who live in civilized lands have more opportunities for education than have those in less privileged countries. We learned early to read the Bible, but in spite of this, do we neglect it?

Do not neglect the most important preparation for your busy day. Start it with God; close it with God; and spend the hours in between in fellowship with Him.

A Final Tip

If you find that you neglect things
Pray to God, and then expect things.

17

KENT A. FORDIT
(Can't afford it)

A Bible Tip

II Corinthians 8:1-12

A Memory Tip

"But this I say, He which soweth sparingly shall reap also sparingly; and he which soweth bountifully shall reap also bountifully. Every man according as he purposeth in his heart, so let him give; not grudgingly, or of necessity: for God loveth a cheerful giver" (II Cor. 9:6,7).

A Timely Tip

In Old Testament days, our Lord provided the people with 100 per cent of their needs, and only asked that 10 per cent be returned to Him. Do you suppose some of the people of that day said, "But we can't afford it"? We would think it strange if that were true. God provided the 100 and only asked the 10. Why should they say they couldn't afford it? It wasn't really theirs. It was His.

But the same is true today. God provides for us 100 per cent. He has given us work, clothing, homes, families, churches, schools, and all of our other needs. Then He asks of us just a small share; perhaps a part of our lives. Perhaps He asks for some of our money or talent. But we say, "I can't afford it."

Hundreds of non-giving Christians have found that they can't afford *not* to give, and have changed their methods and ways. Baby sitters have given God a share; paper carriers have held out God's part first. Some with no employment have given themselves to a prayer life. In each case God has abundantly blessed.

You say you can't afford to give God a part? You can't afford not to! If you say you belong to Him, then so does your money, your time, your effort, your strength, your vitality, your all.

But your school work, your sports activities take too much time? You have nothing left for Him? The Bible says, "Seek ye first the kingdom of God" and again "Seek those things which are above." You can't afford not to.

A Final Tip
Give the Lord His rightful share,
Whether time or gifts or prayer.

18

FAYE KING
(Faking)

A Bible Tip

Psalm 1

A Memory Tip

"Be merciful unto me, O Lord: for I cry unto thee daily" (Ps. 86:3).

A Timely Tip

A great pianist once said, "If I neglect to practice one day, I would notice it. If I miss two days, my friends would notice it, but if I miss more than that, the whole world would notice it."

If every Christian young person would think of his spiritual life in this same way, there would be a revival in every school and city in our land. What you are shows up every day. Your fellow students know whether you are a fake or are sincere.

If you neglect to read God's Word one day, you notice it. If you neglect to read it two days, no doubt your close friends will notice it; but if you neglect to

42

read God's Word and spend time in prayer day after day, the world around you will soon notice it.

There is nothing worse than a fake Christian; and the fellow or girl who does not know Christ can point out a fake everytime. "He's no better than I am," he says, and he may be right.

An anxious mother was waiting for some word from her husband who had gone to war, but no word came. One day her little girl said, "Mother, why don't we pray?"

"I don't know how," confessed the mother. "I have never prayed."

"I do," said the little girl. "All you do is tell God."

Yes, all we have to do is "tell God." Tell Him what is on our hearts; what our needs are for that day.

God's way of talking to us is through His Word. Our way of talking to Him is by prayer. It is something you need to do daily. If you neglect it, you will soon notice it, your friends will soon notice it, and others will soon notice it, too.

A Final Tip

A day of quiet time you've skipped?
It's like a soldier half-equipped.

19

MYRA CULLS
(Miracles)

A Bible Tip
Psalm 8:1-9

A Memory Tip
"Ah Lord God! Behold, thou hast made the heaven and the earth by thy great power and stretched out arm, and there is nothing too hard for thee" (Jer. 32:17).

A Timely Tip
Have you ever noticed that when God does something, He so often does it in a spectacular way?

He takes tiny drops of water and with them makes the rivers and oceans. Men build boats and ships to sail the seas, but only God can make the water.

God makes the air and the sky. Men make airplanes; but they can fly only as they conform to God's laws for flying.

God takes a little watermelon seed and uses His own created sunshine and rain, and causes that seed to increase its own weight 200,000 times. The result: a big watermelon. Men not only enjoy the delicious taste of the melon, but some of them take as much credit for planting the seed as though they were its creator. Yet, without the work of God there would be neither seed nor harvest.

God formed the sky and placed in it the beautiful moon, the shining stars, and the brilliant sun. Only God could do all these things.

Man's inventions and works do not last long. God's created things have been working perfectly since they were first begun. They are beyond the wisdom and understanding of man, but so often man tries to take the credit, when the credit belongs only to God.

But outstanding among God's wonderful creations and miracles is His salvation for sinful man. God created man, put him on this specially created earth and gave him all he could desire. Then man sinned. He deserved death and hell, but God came to the rescue and provided a Sacrifice — a way of escape in the Person of His Son, Jesus Christ.

God's greatest creation is man, and His greatest miracle or marvel is providing salvation for this sinful being.

Truly, we can lift our hearts and voices with the song writer and sing, "What a wonderful Saviour is Jesus my Lord!"

A Final Tip

The days of miracles aren't done,
Salvation's work has just begun.

20

IMA LOKINUP
(I'm looking up)

A Bible Tip
John 14:1-6

A Memory Tip
"If ye then be risen with Christ, seek those things which are above, where Christ sitteth on the right hand of God. Set your affection on things above, not on things on the earth" (Col. 3:1,2).

A Timely Tip
A mother had been reading to her four-year-old boy about Heaven. She read story after story from a Bible story book and from God's Word also. Without the mother fully realizing it, these stories were making a deep impression on her young son. As storytime was over, the mother and son knelt for their customary prayer time. Ordinarily the young boy prayed for his mother and father, his playmates, and about the things that had taken place that day. But this time the little

boy prayed, "Lord Jesus, please come and take me home to heaven, right now, because I can't wait."

For a moment there was a real lump in the mother's throat. She had wanted to impress the boy with the beauties of Heaven and with the fact that God was there, and that someday we who knew and loved the Lord Jesus would go there to be with Him. But now as he prayed, she wondered if she would be willing to part with her son if God chose to take him home, as he was requesting.

The more she thought about it, the more her heart was filled with happiness, because in reading God's Word she had impressed on him that this world was not his home, that heaven was a wonderful place, a home for those who knew and loved the Saviour.

Sometimes we get so occupied in our work, whether it is school or employment (and we seemingly have such a good time here) that we forget this world is not our home.

I wonder, if in child-like faith, with this little boy, we could honestly and sincerely say to the Lord Jesus, "Please come and take me home, because I can't wait. I want to see You right away."

Our thoughts ought always to be centered on Him. And though we live in a busy world, we need to take time to think about our heavenly home.

A Final Tip

My life should have a deep desire
To sing with joy, "I'm Going Higher."

21

HEDDA NOUT
(Heading out)

A Bible Tip

I Samuel 3:1-10

A Memory Tip

"And the work of righteousness shall be peace; and the effect of righteousness quietness and assurance forever" (Isa. 32:17).

A Timely Tip

Going, going, going! twentieth-century young people (their parents too) always seem to be going. They seem to have the idea that sitting still is for the very old people — the rocking chair age, and they want no part in it. From Sunday through Saturday they've got to be on the go.

Activity is certainly not sin, but when activity replaces quiet time and meditation with the Lord, it is wrong.

We live such a hurried, rushed life these days that we seem to have forgotten what the Bible teaches about being quiet. We no longer let God speak to us in an atmosphere that is quiet and peaceful.

The Word of God says, "Be still and know that I am God." It says "sit still" — "be quiet."

When the disciples were out in the middle of the lake and a storm came up, they were greatly agitated as they tried to find a way to escape the danger of the roaring waters. Excitedly they woke Jesus up and said, "Master, carest thou not that we perish?"

Now if this had taken place in our day, we would have rushed around shouting instructions here, there, and everywhere. But Jesus did not become excited because they were excited. He quietly arose and said, "Peace, be still." The storm ended right then.

We need to learn that we do not need to live in a rushing, noisy atmosphere. The peace of God needs to control our lives. We need to walk softly and live quietly before Him. Our lives are hid with Christ, in God, and we must take time to be with Him.

If we were with some members of a royal family, we would be so highly honored that we would want to spend as much time as possible with them. It would be disgraceful to hurry around nervously in their presence. So, with the Lord Jesus, we must not be hurried or rushed or noisy, but live quietly and peacefully, enjoying His presence.

A Final Tip

A daily, quiet time I'll seek,
Not only in my church each week.

22

MAE DONEROR
(Made an error)

A Bible Tip

Proverbs 14:12-16

A Memory Tip

"All the ways of a man are clean in his own eyes; but the Lord weigheth the spirits. Commit thy works unto the Lord, and thy thoughts shall be established" (Prov. 16:2,3).

A Timely Tip

A young girl went to visit a sick woman in the neighborhood. Each time she went, her mother would send some cookies or flowers with her.

One day the little girl decided that she wanted to bring her own gift, not something her mother had sent. On the way from school that afternoon she saw a beautiful strawberry patch. It almost looked as though they were growing wild, but there was a fence around the patch, so she knew it belonged to the farm on the other side of the road. She looked all around before climbing the fence to be sure no one would see her, then she began to fill her lunch box. Every now and then she would put one in her mouth and smile at the sweet taste. How Mrs. Evans would enjoy these strawberries. That evening she delivered the berries to the sick lady. "I picked them just for you," she said proudly.

"How sweet of you," said Mrs. Evans. "You certainly sacrificed to get these didn't you?"

"No," said the girl, "it was no sacrifice; they were easy to get."

"But," said the lady, "you got poison ivy in picking them."

The startled girl looked down at her legs and there were the indications of poison ivy. It was going to be hard to explain to Mrs. Evans and to her mother that she had stolen the berries, but she would have to do it.

Sometimes our thoughts for others are right. We want to do something for them, but in our enthusiasm, we sin, because we do things in our own way.

No doubt, the farmer would have given the girl permission to pick the berries, warning her of the poison ivy in the area if she had asked.

Her motive was right, but her method was wrong. We must be careful so that both motive and method are of the Lord.

A Final Tip

Sometimes a wrong may seem so right,
But it is sin in Jesus' sight.

23

ERNEST N. ALTHINGZ
(Earnest in all things)

A Bible Tip

Acts 18:24-28

A Memory Tip

"And whatsoever ye do in word or deed, do all in the name of the Lord Jesus, giving thanks to God and the Father by him" (Col. 3:17).

A Timely Tip

Many years ago, after Dwight L. Moody had accepted Christ as his Saviour, he wanted to teach a Sunday school class. He went to the superintendent and asked for a class, but the superintendent suggested that he go out and get his own. Moody did this. He brought in boys from the streets and began faithfully to teach them from the Word of God. Through this, Mr. Moody led all his boys to the Lord Jesus.

During the ministry of Charles Spurgeon, one of the members of his church was asked to teach the senior women in the Sunday school. It was just a small class, but it needed a teacher who would faithfully teach them the things of the Lord. At first, the class consisted of less than six members.

After a few months of hard work, it had grown to fifty, and before long it was necessary to hold the class sessions in a larger room. Soon after going into this room, some 300 women were attending regularly, and after only one year with this teacher, some 500 women were in attendance in the class.

This woman continued her work, until more than 800 women met every week to study the Word of God. From this class went out scores of other Sunday school teachers and church workers, all through the faithfulness of one woman — Mrs. Bartlett.

When God gives you a task to do, do it sincerely. Do it with all the power and stamina you have. Don't go "haphazard" on Him. Give Him your best, whether it is teaching a Sunday school class, picking up kids to go to church, cleaning the church basement, or making cookies for the VBS class.

You are just as responsible to God for your job as Dwight L. Moody was for the boys in his class, or Mrs. Bartlett was for her 800 Bible students.

Whatever you do, do it to the very best of your ability; then God will increase and bless it.

A Final Tip

When God asks you to produce,
Don't come up with some excuse.

24

Y. GOTA CHURCH
(Why go to church)

A Bible Tip
Psalm 84:1-12

A Memory Tip
"Not forsaking the assembling of ourselves together, as the manner of some is; but exhorting one another: and so much the more, as ye see the day approaching" (Heb. 10:25).

A Timely Tip
Sometimes young people ask, "Is it necessary to go to church in order to be a true Christian?" Well, we must admit that attending church will not save a person, nor does merely attending services make one a better Christian.

Then why go? Why not take Sunday morning as a sleep-in day, a time to read the paper, check the news, get caught up on rest, and use the day for just taking things easy?

There are some good reasons for attending church.

The Word of God tells us that we should meet together to have fellowship with people of like precious faith. It's a little hard for you to do this if you are going to be at your house and the others at God's house.

God has ordained ministers to preach the Gospel, and to shepherd the church. Therefore, it's a pretty good idea for a fellow or a girl to remember that Sunday is the Lord's day, a time when Christians ought to be in His house. This in itself is a witness for our Lord.

More and more it seems that the people of the world are planning sports activities such as golf, baseball, tennis, and ever so many other things on the Lord's day. They will do almost anything to lure young people away from God's house. But we who know and love the Saviour ought to be very careful not to waste this day in trivialities, but rather use it to worship the Saviour.

By attending a church where the Gospel is preached, we obey the Lord. We also fellowship with fellow Christians, and learn more about our Saviour. In pooling their resources of money, time, talents, and service, a group of Christians can do much more to spread the gospel than if just one tried to do the work alone.

A Final Tip

Worship God and go to church,
For there the Word of God you'll search.

25

I. KENT DOIT
(I can't do it)

A Bible Tip

Psalm 23

A Memory Tip

Thy word is a lamp unto my feet, and a light unto my path" (Ps. 119:105).

A Timely Tip

A traveler who had to go on a long and dangerous journey over a rugged and dangerous mountain, was not sure he knew the way. So he stopped at an information booth and asked the consultant about the road. The travel expert showed him on the map the best way to go. He pointed out the roads clearly and distinctly and told him the pitfalls he should watch out for.

So the traveler went his way. As he continued his journey, he found that the rocks grew more treacherous and the way seemed to be more lonely. Finally, he became very discouraged and cried out loudly:

"It is impossible for a man to go on such a path or climb these rocks."

Suddenly, he heard a kind voice calling, "Take courage young man, just follow me."

As the traveler looked around, he saw the man who had pointed out the correct road to him. This was the man who had also given him the map, warned him of the ravines and the precipices, and pointed out the beauties of the trip.

New courage came to the traveler as he began to follow his leader, and before night they reached the top of the mountain.

God's Word is our map. It points out the way for us to go. It shows that we will find steep mountains and ravines, and also some precipices. There will be dark clouds and thunderstorms and other difficulties. But we will also find beautiful valleys, flowers, and rainbows.

So you begin your journey, and just about the time you are ready to throw up your hands and cry, "It can't be done, it can't be done," you hear God's voice saying, "I'm just ahead of you; follow Me."

A Final Tip

When the Bible is your map,
There's less danger of mishap.

26

ANN REMBRANTZ
(In remembrance)

A Bible Tip

I Corinthians 11:23-34

A Memory Tip

"And he took bread, and gave thanks, and brake it, and gave unto them, saying, This is my body which is given for you: this do in remembrance of me. Likewise also the cup after supper, saying, This cup is the new testament in my blood, which is shed for you" (Luke 22:19,20).

A Timely Tip

A young teen-age girl stood at the bedside of her dying mother. In utter weakness, the mother slipped off the diamond ring from her finger and gave it to her daughter.

"Wear this, honey," she said in a whisper, "and always think of me when you do."

Do you think this young girl ever forgot her mother? I am sure that every time she looked down at her hand

and saw the beautiful diamond ring, a memorial to her mother, she remembered that dying wish: "Wear this and remember me." No doubt, whenever she was tempted to do wrong, the beautiful gem would seem to sparkle a little brighter and she would remember.

Our Lord Jesus has given us a dying wish, too. In speaking of the solemnity of the communion table, our Saviour said, "This do in remembrance of me."

Some young people do not seem to know the real meaning of communion. It may be held weekly, monthly, or quarterly in your church, but each time it is a memorial to the Saviour.

If you have put your trust in the Lord Jesus as Saviour, that is, if you are truly His child, then you should seek to take part in the communion service, for He has commanded you to do so: "This *do*" is what He said. Be sure, of course, and discuss this with your pastor.

Every time we read or hear those familiar verses, every time we see the communion table, our hearts and minds ought to become very serious as we think of His broken body; His shed blood; His death; His burial, and His resurrection for us.

Communion day is a memorial day for every Christian. Jesus not only said, "THIS DO," but He said, "This do in REMEMBRANCE OF ME."

A Final Tip

Memorial day now growing dim?
You'd better get your eyes on Him.

27

VAL. U. OVASOLE
(Value of a soul)

A Bible Tip
Isaiah 50-2-10

A Memory Tip
"But ye shall receive power, after that the Holy
Ghost is come upon you: and ye shall be witnesses
unto me both in Jerusalem, and in all Judaea, and in
Samaria, and unto the uttermost part of the earth"
(Acts 1:8).

A Timely Tip
There was a great deal of commotion on board ship!
"Man overboard," cried one of the sailors! It seemed
that everyone on the ship gathered on the deck. The
heartbeat of the people quickened as they saw a young
man going down. In just a moment a life belt was
thrown out, for the poor victim did not know how to
swim. But he was not able to get his hands on it. Up
came the boy's head, down it went again. People were

screaming! Some were praying, "God, save this boy." Some were almost in panic over the incident.

As the young boy came up for the second time, a sailor jumped overboard to rescue the struggling lad. But because the boy was so frightened, he fought, and in this way made the rescue more difficult. With all the energy the sailor had, he finally rescued the young man; but in his effort, the brave navy man lost his own life.

Some of our friends are in that same lost condition. They are drowning because of sin. They have gone down for the second time, and unless we jump in to rescue them now, they will be lost; eternally lost. But in it all, there seems to be so little concern on our part. We stand on the deck and cry with the mob, "Man overboard, man overboard!" But we do little or nothing to rescue him. No one seems willing to jump into the water and save him. No one really cares if he goes down for the third time, or if he is rescued. And, as he sinks beneath the water of sin, the crowd on the deck turns and says, "Too bad; too bad!"

Is that all the soul of a person means to you? Or are you willing to rescue him? Even at the cost of your own life? Remember, Christ gave His for us all. Physical death is dark, but spiritual death is even darker. What are you doing for your unsaved friends?

A Final Tip

Drowning people have no hope;
Won't you give the lifeline rope?

28

HAL P. AFREND
(Help a friend)

A Bible Tip

Matthew 5:13-16

A Memory Tip

"But be ye doers of the word, and not hearers only, deceiving your own selves" (James 1:22).

A Timely Tip

Some of the farmers in the community had been praying for Farmer Smith for a long time. He seemed to be the only one in the area who did not believe in the Lord Jesus Christ. Members and friends of the church had prayed earnestly for his salvation. The deacons and the pastor had talked to him; but for some reason, Farmer Smith did not see the need of giving his heart to Christ.

"I get along pretty well without God," he said. "I've had a bigger crop than most of you men every year."

But then, shortly before harvest time Farmer Smith took deathly sick. He was rushed to the hospital in town, and for many days lay between life and death. As soon as he regained consciousness, the pastor of the church came to talk with him.

"I know what you are going to say," said Farmer Smith. "You are going to tell me that I need God. But I can't believe in Him now," continued the farmer bitterly. "Look at what He did to me. Just at harvest time He knocked me down. Now I'll lose all of my crop. What will happen to my family?"

"No," said the pastor, "God didn't let you down and neither did God's people." He then went on to tell the farmer how the men of the community had already harvested his crop, and now they were doing their own.

The sick farmer was so surprised at the love of his neighbors that he had to admit, "That's real Christianity." As a result, he gave his heart and life to Christ.

Sometimes our unsaved loved ones cannot see Christ except through what we do and how we live. Their slowness to respond may tempt us to be discouraged, but God is working in their hearts through our lives.

God has not asked us to save souls. He has merely asked us to witness and to live before our friends in a way that He can work the miracles in the hearts and lives of these unsaved people.

A Final Tip

Actions often speak quite loud,
Make an impact on the crowd.

29

CHICK N. HARTED
(Chicken hearted)

A Bible Tip

Joshua 1:1-9

A Memory Tip

"Prove all things; hold fast that which is good. Abstain from all appearance of evil" (I. Thess. 5:21,22).

A Timely Tip

No doubt, you've heard the term "chicken" used for the person who does not dare or care to do something. If he won't go along with the gang, he's considered chicken. If he won't play rought, he's chicken. If he won't pick up a dare, he's chicken.

But some people are known to be cowardly, weak, pliable, and easily led simply because they do not have enough courage to stand up for what they really believe. They will do almost anything the gang tells them to do. They definitely know the difference between right and wrong, but because they are afraid to differ from the majority, or the crowd, they go along with the suggestion which often leads them into sin. It may start very innocently, but it often leads to something bigger and bigger.

That's the way it was with a fellow named Chick. It all started when the fellows talked him into skipping the Sunday evening service and ended when he was with a bunch of fellows who robbed the local drive-in. No, he didn't commit the burglary; he just sat in the car, but he was an accomplice. Oh, yes, he knew it was wrong. But he wasn't going to be called a chicken or a coward, so he went along. He wasn't too chicken to do it! He was too chicken to refuse!

God needs strong, stalwart young men. He needs fellows and girls who dare to say "no" when "no" needs to be said. Or "yes" when "yes" needs to be said. He needs young people who aren't afraid to face the truth and the right. Are you that type of person?

If you are a Christian, determine in your heart to live and move in the strength of the Lord rather than your own.

A Final Tip

When your backbone isn't strong,
You'll be tempted to do wrong.

30

VERA E. SMALL
(Very Small)

A Bible Tip
I John 3:4-10

A Memory Tip

"Jesus answered them, Verily, verily, I say unto you, Whosoever committeth sin is the servant of sin" (John 8:34).

A Timely Tip

Vera was the kind of Christian who thought it was perfectly all right to commit what she called little sins if she did not do them often. In other words, her attitude seemed to be that some sins were not so bad if she did not indulge in them constantly.

There are many Christian young people just like Vera. But these are not the ones who are wholly dedicated to the Saviour.

Let's stop and think about this. Are sins wrong only when they are big? Are they sin only if they are done often?

There is hardly any weight or size to one grain of sand, but have you tried to lift a barrel full?

A grain of salt seems so small and insignificant, but if all the salt in the sea was piled up it would make mountains.

One drop of water is almost nothing, but drop upon drop upon drop makes an ocean.

One small thread is hardly strong enough to hold a button to your clothing, but many threads fasten it securely to the garment.

One small sin may seem insignificant, but sin upon sin in a person's life becomes very degrading. Before you know it, the sin has conquered you, and has control of your life. Perhaps the first drink of liquor did not make a drunkard out of a man or woman, but habitual drinking soon did.

When we fail to look on sin as sin, we become slaves to sin, and no longer live an effective, victorious life. We, cannot, under such a condition, be good witnesses for our Lord. When we sin, we should come to the Lord immediately to ask for forgiveness, freedom, and victory. Read I John 1:9 for more help on this.

A Final Tip

It may begin with just a tinge,
But soon it makes the victim cringe.

31

SERCHA SONGBOK
(Search a songbook)

A Bible Tip
I Chronicles 16:23-29

A Memory Tip
"That thou mayest know how thou oughtest to behave thyself in the house of God, which is the church of the living God, the pillar and ground of the truth" (I Tim. 3:15).

A Timely Tip
Some teen-agers have the habit of going through the church hymnal page by page and checking the titles during the service. When they do this, they miss the message of the congregational singing, the pastoral prayer, the announcements, the choral number, and the ministry from the Word. All because their attention was on flipping pages in the hymnbook, rather than on the message.

I have seen young people take the book and go from title to title to try to make an interesting story. The result? The shaking of the pew, and a giggle from the group that disturbed the entire service. The people seated around them, people who came to hear the Word, were unable to do so because of this disturbance.

If you must search the songbook, why not do it to get a message — but not during church service! Get a group of fellows and girls together sometime, open the hymnbooks, take the titles, and read them carefully and prayerfully. Then go through each song, verse by verse. You just might get something for your spiritual life. You might even be able to lead one of the kids to the Lord.

Go over the words to "Just As I Am," "Take My Life," "I Surrender All," "Jesus, I Come," "Let Him In," "Onward Christian Soldiers," "When I Survey the Wondrous Cross" and others. The next time these songs are sung in church, you will find they have a deeper meaning than ever before. You will find the message of the composer and the poet gripping your own heart. You will find they aren't just words on page, and notes on a staff.

Many persons have confessed that it was the song, "Just As I Am," that God used to speak to their hearts for salvation. And, "I'll Go Where You Want Me to Go," has decided many to go to the uttermost parts of the world.

Yes, go ahead, search the songbook, but search it for a message.

A Final Tip

Want to make the message stick?
When you read it, make it click.

32

CECIL U. DUE
(Sees all you do)

A Bible Tip
Hebrews 4:12-16

A Memory Tip
"For the ways of man are before the eyes of the Lord, and he pondereth all his goings" (Prov. 5:21).

A Timely Tip
A man who didn't have a very good crop on his farm looked with envy over at his neighbor's corn field. There, he saw a very wonderful crop. One day he decided he would sneak over there and steal some of the corn. He took his little boy with him and told the boy to keep a lookout all around the field, and give his father warning in case anyone should come along.

Quickly the man opened the sack he had brought with him. First he looked one way, then another. When it was quite evident that there was no one around, he began to fill the sack with his neighbor's corn. Just as he dropped the first ear of corn in the old sack, his little boy cried out, "Father, there is one way you haven't looked yet."

Immediately the father stopped. He took a step closer to the place where his son was standing, and looked about, almost expecting to see someone coming.

"Where?" he called.

The little boy looked at his father and said calmly: "You forgot to look up."

The father was so conscience-stricken that he dropped the sack, took his little boy by the hand, and returned home — without his neighbor's corn.

The Scriptures tell us that "a little child shall lead them." This has often been the case. A young child can sometimes reach the heart of his father when no one else is able to do so.

We, too, can learn from those who are younger than we — younger in years, and younger in the faith. The father thought he had looked in every direction, but he had forgotten the most important way — up.

When you are tempted to do something wrong; when you think you will not be seen by anyone, remember to take one more look — up. If you do this, chances are you will not commit the sin.

A Final Tip

Are you prone to slip in sin?
Stop; apply God's discipline.

33

ADA ZIRE
(A desire)

A Bible Tip

Genesis 50:15-21

A Memory Tip

"Moreover as for me, God forbid that I should sin against the Lord in ceasing to pray for you: but I will teach you the good and the right way" (I Sam. 12:23).

A Timely Tip

A little boy was saying his prayers one night. After he had thanked the Lord for everything that day, he ended it with the usual, "God bless Mother and Daddy and Susie. Amen." He was just about to jump into bed when he got back down on his knees and said, "Never mind Susie, God. I forgot, I'm mad at her."

This may seem like a very childish action, but sometimes it is done by teen-agers and older people, as well. Oh, it may not be in just those words, but our hearts and actions tell the story.

Sometimes we refuse to pray for those who treat us

wrongly. Sometimes we even refuse to pray for those who do not know our Saviour just because they are not particularly friendly to us.

When God reminds us to pray for a certain person, we are responsible for that individual. We must pray for him as though he were the last sheep to be found, and we were responsible to get him into the fold. We should be so concerned for these unsaved people, that we would even be willing to give our own lives, if necessary, in order to see them saved.

But so often we let personal gripes and grudges get between us and the salvation of our friends and family.

Do you have an unsaved mother or father, sister or brother, relative or friend? Is there something in your actions that is keeping that one from coming to the Lord? Are you a hindrance rather than a help in his salvation?

Perhaps you would never say with your lips, "Oh, never mind Susie, Lord. I'm mad at her," but your actions prove to the Lord that this is exactly what your heart is saying. Examine yourself and see if you are the reason your friends and family do not know your Saviour.

A Final Tip

Christian actions immature?
Read God's Word and grow, for sure.

34

ONA LEE WONWAY
(Only one way)

A Bible Tip
Isaiah 55:1-11

A Memory Tip

"O Jerusalem, Jerusalem, which killest the prophets, and stonest them that are sent unto thee; how often would I have gathered thy children together, as a hen doth gather her brood under her wings, and ye would not" (Luke 13:34).

A Timely Tip

A young man was stricken with a serious blood disease. He was told that science had recently discovered a medicine for this disease, but rather than calling his doctor in order to obtain the medicine, he sent his friends to the library to get all the books they could find describing the disease. The next several days the young man spent all his time and effort reading the books which told about this blood disease. But in spite of all his reading, the young man died within a few days, because the dreaded disease had gripped his entire body.

No doubt, you say, "How foolish! Why didn't he take the medicine that had been discovered for just such a disease? He should have known that books would not help him."

We see the foolishness of this man, and yet people today do the same thing for their spiritual sicknesses. They read books about God and books about what He has done. Some of them even read the Book of books, the Bible, in order to learn more about creation, and other interesting facts, but they fail to get the most important message, because they refuse to take the one cure — the blood of Jesus Christ.

They go to church; they put some of their money in the offering plate; they sing the hymns; they like the atmosphere of God's house, but they do not want a finger pointed at the disease which is gnawing at their souls. As a result, they die an eternal death.

"How foolish," we say, "when God has made a way." Yes, how foolish indeed! Have you accepted God's cure for sin? If so, have your friends found this ONLY way — the Lord Jesus Christ?

A Final Tip

He's the remedy for sin,
Directions say, "Just let Him in."

35

POP U. LARITY
(Popularity)

A Bible Tip
Proverbs 3:3-7

A Memory Tip
"A good name is rather to be chosen than great riches, and loving favor rather than silver and gold" (Prov. 22:1).

A Timely Tip
Did you ever try to figure out what popularity really was? It seems to be something young people want, desire, crave, and fight for, but what is it? What does a popular kid have that everybody likes? On what is it based?

Certainly it includes respect and sincerity. Nobody likes a fake. They like someone who is genuine, sincere, and real. Take a quick look at those who are considered popular in school, in church, in town. Are they big blows, fakes, or cover-ups? Not as a rule. They generally act very normal, never too high or too low, just on the norm.

On the other hand, what about the fellow or girl who isn't popular? He is always pretending to be something or someone he isn't. No doubt, you have met people who came from the middlewest who suddenly developed a definite western "twang" in their speech. Or someone from the East who tries to talk like a southerner. Some teens add a lisp to their speech because somebody who is real cute does it. Hairdos, wardrobes, record files, book shelves, and "what have you" follow with the trends of popularity.

But the most important question is not, are you popular with the gang? but rather, are you popular with God? Does He know you? Does He recognize the real you? Are you sincere and genuine when you come to Him? or are you a fake?

When you realize that you are going into the very presence of God, the Creator, the Redeemer, the Saviour, the Father, the King of kings, are you sincere? Are you honest? Are you just saying a group of words? or do you really talk with Him?

If you insist on being popular, make your popularity count with God.

A Final Tip

Your friends may often laugh or sneer.
But just hold fast and be sincere.

36

WENDY WANDIT
(When he wanted it)

A Bible Tip
Psalm 34:17-22

A Memory Tip

"And Jesus said unto them... If ye have faith as a grain of mustard seed, ye shall say unto this mountain, Remove hence to yonder place; and it shall remove; and nothing shall be impossible unto you" (Matt. 17:20).

A Timely Tip

Many years ago, in Germany, a young husband and wife learned that God never fails to provide, and at just the moment when it is most needed.

There was no money in the house. A piece of cloth had been ordered from the weaver, and it was to be delivered that night. There was no one in the village from whom the man could borrow the money. Up to this point he had kept it a secret, but now he knew he would have to tell his wife. She burst into tears as he told her that there was no money for the cloth.

"But our Heavenly Father will provide," he finished. "Maybe we will have bad weather, and the weaver will not be able to come today."

Together the husband and wife knelt and committed their problem to the Lord, for they knew there was no human help.

Early that evening the wife burst into the study where her husband had gone to read. "The weaver is here," she cried. At that very moment the husband was taking a book from the shelf. As he took the book, a piece of money rolled out and fell rattling on the table. Both the husband and wife stood staring at the money. God had known their problem, and He had known the very moment the money would be needed.

After the weaver had left the piece of cloth and had gone, the husband and wife remembered how they had placed the money in the book months before.

God always provides. He does not leave His children helpless. Sometimes we try to make God fit into our pattern. But God's ways are not our ways, and our ways are not God's ways. When He has promised to "supply all our needs according to His riches in glory by Christ Jesus," we must learn to trust and believe.

A Final Tip
Not too early, not too late
God provides, if we but wait.

37

EVY DENSE
(Evidence)

A Bible Tip

Psalm 51:1-12

A Memory Tip

"He that covereth his sins shall not prosper: but whoso confesseth and forsaketh them shall have mercy" (Prov. 28:13).

A Timely Tip

Many years ago a plantation owner called all his slaves together and announced that he had been robbed.

"One of you is guilty," he said, "and I know which one." For a moment there was a tense quietness among the group. "I had a dream last night," continued the owner, "and in my dream I saw the robber. Then I heard a voice that said, 'The one who has robbed you will have a small feather light upon his nose.'"

Just as the plantation owner finished telling about his dream, one of the slaves impulsively brushed his finger across his nose. The owner looked at him and said, "You are the guilty one, aren't you?" The slave admitted his theft.

Sometimes when the contents of the cookie bowl seems to be going down faster than it should, Mother calls the children together and says, "Somebody is eating too many cookies, and I think I know just who it is. The crumbs around your mouth reveal the truth." With a sweep of the hand the guilty one tries to brush off the evidence, and Mother knows immediately who it is.

When God looks at His children, He says, "You have sinned, your heart and life show it." And with the same quick impulse that the slave had when he tried to brush off the feather, and with the same sweep of motion that the cookie snatcher used to cover up his theft, so we try to cover up the stain. But God says, "You are the one. The evidence is here."

God's Word does not lie. We cannot get away with sin. We are guilty before Almighty God, and we must confess our sins in order to have a clean heart and life.

A Final Tip

Covering sin could make you sick,
Because it makes your conscience prick.

38

ANN EMY ATAKS
(Enemy attacks)

A Bible Tip

Ephesians 6:10-18

A Memory Tip

"And the Lord said, Simon, Simon, behold, Satan
hath desired to have you, that he may sift you as wheat:
But I have prayed for thee, that thy faith fail not: and
when thou art converted, strengthen thy brethren"
(Luke 22:31,32).

A Timely Tip

Years ago when wars were fought around the walls
of a city, the conqueror would be victorious only when
he was able to knock down these walls, and take over
the city. But before the enemy would call his men to go
and fight the people of that city, he would first sent
spies to find the weakest part of the wall.

So it is in any kind of struggle. The enemy looks
for the shallowest part of the river, the lowest part of
the gate, the weakest point in the wall. His spies have

examined every inch in the area, and when the city seems to be asleep, and when the people least expect it, with great force the enemy attacks and captures the entire city.

So the Devil goes around seeking whom he may devour. He tests the Christian to find his weakness. Is he apt to sin when he is physically tired? Hungry? Discouraged? Mentally depressed? Poverty stricken? When studies are too much for him? When grades seem to drop? When everything seems to go wrong?

When Satan finds the weakness, he watches, and watches, and watches; then he attacks. He strikes! And if we are off guard, he captures and conquers.

Unless we are living close to the Lord Jesus, spending much time in His Word, and talking the whole situation over with Him, we are apt to be captured; we are likely to fall.

In Ephesians 5:13, we read, "Wherefore take unto you the whole armour of God, that ye may be able to withstand in the evil day, and having done all, to stand."

A Final Tip

Guard yourself from Satan's dart,
Aimed to pierce the Christian's heart.

39

I. B. LEVINHIM
(I believe in Him)

A Bible Tip

Isaiah 40:25-28

A Memory Tip

"He hath made every thing beautiful in his time: also he hath set the world in their heart, so that no man can find out the work that God maketh from the beginning to the end" (Eccles. 3:11).

A Timely Tip

A minister once asked an old negro man what his reasons were for believing in the existence of God.

"Sir," said the negro, "I have been here many, many years. Every day since I have been in this world, I have seen the sun rise in the east and set in the west. The North star stands where it did the first time I ever saw it. The seven stars in Job's coffin keep on the same path in the sky and never turn out.

"It ain't so with man's works. He makes clocks and watches and they may run for a little while, but soon they get out of fix and the clock stands still. Man makes automobiles and they have flat tires and motor trouble. Seems everything man makes needs a lot of fixing all the time.

"God's sun and moon and stars keep on shining the same way all the time. God's power makes one man die and another one get well. He sends the rain and the sun and always keeps everything in motion. Why, how can I help but believe in that kind of God?"

In schools today, young people are confronted with almost every type of teaching. They hear theories of evolution and teachings of a non-existent god. Atheism and other forms of unbelief that could shake their faith, are presented as though they were true.

But the God in whom we believe, the True and Living One, not only created the entire universe, but continues to keep it in motion. Have you ever noticed that it is never in need of repairs? We cannot help but believe in such a God.

Man's works are temporary, but God's are eternal. I believe in this God. Do you?

A Final Tip
God's creations last forever;
Man's inventions break and sever.

40

BEA ONGARD
(Be on guard)

A Bible Tip
John 17:9-15

A Memory Tip

"For there shall arise false Christs, and false prophets, and shall shew great signs and wonders; insomuch that, if it were possible, they shall deceive the very elect" (Matt. 24:24).

A Timely Tip

It is said of the African buffalo that his sight allows him to see only those things directly ahead of him, that is, straight forward, but nothing from either the right or the left side. In those areas, things are completely dark.

Sometimes after certain eye surgery a person finds that his vision has changed. He sees clearly as long as the object is directly in front of him. But sometimes there is complete darkness on both sides.

The Christian who does not have perfect spiritual vision is subject to satanic attack. When Satan knows that there is blindness on either or both sides, he comes in from that angle and attacks. He does not come in from the front, for then his actions would be seen.

Unless we are on guard constantly, this side-attack can cause great defeat in our spiritual lives. We may think it is enough to keep looking forward, but we must have spiritual vision for things all around us.

Unless the person who has had eye surgery recognizes that there is darkness on the side and keeps alert for danger, he may be subject to real tragedy. If he cannot see traffic coming from either way, he will find it very difficult to cross a busy street alone. But if he has someone help him, the danger is lessened to a great extent.

If we are not alert to our own weaknesses, we very likely will not see the oncoming attacks of Satan and be on guard against them. Therefore, we must do as the song writers have put it, and "Lean on the everlasting arms of Jesus." As long as we are there, we are "Safe in the Arms of Jesus," and there, we will be "Resting in the Shelter of His Love."

A Final Tip

Dangers lurk on every side,
But I am safe, when He's my Guide.

41

MAY DITABUTY
(Made it a beauty)

A Bible Tip

Hebrews 12:5-11

A Memory Tip

"We are the clay, and thou our potter; and we all are the work of thy hand" (Isa. 64:8). "Shall the thing formed say to him that formed it, Why hast thou made me thus? Hath not the potter power over the clay..." (Rom. 9:20,21).

A Timely Tip

Have you ever watched a ceramist take a mold and pour some clay into it? After the clay has stood in the mold for a time, it begins to take form and become more firm. As the piece is taken out of the mold, you see that it has taken on the exact form of the mold, but it has also taken on some extra lines and creases. When the piece is dry the ceramist takes a knife, a sponge and some water, and begins to smooth out these places. When this is done to his satisfaction, the clay object is placed in the kiln, and fired under intense heat. But not until it is glazed and fired for the second time does it really become a piece of beauty.

The clay itself was not beautiful, nor was the piece taken from the mold, though certainly more shapely. After it was scraped and smoothed, it was better, but still not complete. The first firing improved it; but not until the product had gone through all the firing, and taken on a beautiful glazed finish could it be called an item of beauty.

Now what would have happened if the clay could have talked? As it was poured into the mold, it might have said, "I don't want to be formed this way." Or when it was taken out, and smoothed and scraped, it might have cried, "This hurts, leave me alone." Or as it was put into the kiln to be fired, it could have screamed, "This burns! Take me out!" If it had, it never would have become a thing of beauty. It would always have been in the form of useless clay.

We sometimes respond this way when the Lord wants to make us spiritually beautiful. We need to be molded, but we complain. We need to be formed and made smooth, but we call out: "This hurts." We need to be put into the fire and made "a piece of beauty," but we cry, "Why do you always do this to me?"

In order to be a useful, beautiful vessel, all of these things are necessary.

A Final Tip

Want to be a beauty vessel?
When He molds, don't fight or wrestle.

42

FRANK R. INKIND
(Franker than kind)

A Bible Tip

James 3:5-13

A Memory Tip

"If any man among you seem to be religious, and bridleth not his tongue, but deceiveth his own heart, this man's religion is vain" (James 1:26).

A Timely Tip

Being a Christian, and witnessing about Christ to his buddies, was one of the most important things Frank could think to do. He was known for his honesty and his fair dealings, but he was also known for something else — for being "brutally frank."

If Frank had something to say, he said it. He rarely stopped to think if it was an unkind word, or if it would offend or hurt anyone.

"At least they know where I stand," he would brag when anyone talked with him. "I don't beat around the bush. If a fellow asks for an opinion, I give it to him."

All this was true. Frank did these things; but often in his frankness, he hurt someone, and many times it was his mother.

"I thought you said that you were going to patch these jeans," he said curtly. Suddenly he remembered how busy his mother had been. Both of the younger children had broken out with measles, and his older sister had been away at camp.

What Frank did not realize was that he was being a hindrance rather than a testimony to his friends and family.

"If that blabber-mouth is a Christian," said one of the fellows in the neighborhood, "then I'm not sure I care to be one. He is always sticking his nose in somebody else's affairs and giving free advice when it is not needed."

Sometimes we think we are helping when we give our frank opinions and impressions, but it might be better to keep our advice to ourselves unless someone asks for it. Our blunt, brutal, and overly frank impulses need to be committed to the Lord just as well as the grave sins in our lives.

A Final Tip
Think your chatter's good advice?
Better it'd kept on ice.

43

WOODY B. WORLDLEE
(Would be worldly)

A Bible Tip

Matthew 6:19-24

A Memory Tip

"But seek ye first the kingdom of God, and his righteousness; and all these things shall be added unto you" (Matt. 6:33). "If ye then be risen with Christ, seek those things which are above . . . Set your affection on things above, not on things on the earth" (Col. 3:1,2).

A Timely Tip

It has been said that worldly riches are like nuts: many clothes are torn in getting them, many teeth are broken in cracking them, but the body is never filled by eating them.

So often we get our eyes on the wrong things. The school basketball games, the pep club, the school play, or other activities become so important that we neglect spiritual things.

When it comes to school activities our motto seems to be:

> "Live or die
> For Local High."

But when God asks us to put His Word, His work, His worship first, we rebel. We think the minister expects too much from us and the choir director is too demanding. Even the menial tasks become big and difficult.

We spend days and hours tearing our clothes and breaking our teeth to gather nuts of worldly pleasures, and even then, we are not satisfied.

Like the prodigal of old, we spend all we have in riotous living, and when we finally come to ourselves we must admit that we are sinners, not worthy to be called sons. We must repent, turn around, and go back to the Father.

How do you stand when it comes to putting first things first? Are you able to do it cheerfully, or do you grumble, complain, and fuss about having to "give up so much" for the Lord?

Think it over! What things in your life are most important?

A Final Tip

> Things that count must be on top
> All the others then must drop.

44

KENT B. ALEEDER
(Can't be a leader)

A Bible Tip

I Corinthians 12:4-11

A Memory Tip

"Not with eyeservice as menpleasers; but as servants of Christ, doing the will of God from the heart; With good will doing service, as to the Lord, and not to men" (Eph. 6:6,7).

A Timely Tip

Kent was a quiet sort of person, but he had always been active in his young people's society. He had never been chosen president or vice president, but he had been one of the most active workers of the group. He had never taught a Sunday school class or led the opening choruses, and yet it seemed more kids from the Sunday school reported that he had led them to the Lord than almost anyone else.

Kent had quietly gone about his business serving the Lord — visiting children in the neighborhood, talking to them about the Lord Jesus, picking them up in his car, helping in the menial tasks in the church, the Sunday school, and the vacation Bible school.

Sometimes we get the idea that if a fellow is in the background, he isn't really an active worker. We think he has to be on the platform — be a leader or director of some kind. There is usually only one director for each choir, but what would the choir be without the members? There is usually only one teacher for each class, but what would the class be without the members?

All of Jesus' disciples were not leaders; while He was with them He was their leader. Many of them, including the twelve, were of humble background. To them he said, "Follow me," and they obeyed. Some of them became leaders later on, but many of them did not.

He made us what we are. Let us develop our talents to the very best possible degree, giving to Him all we have.

Some must be leaders, but many must be followers. When God prepares a person for a task, no matter what it may be, it is always right.

A Final Tip

If you lead or if you follow
In sin's mire you must not wallow.

45

PHIL D. WITHGOLD
(Filled with gold)

A Bible Tip
Job 23:1-14

A Memory Tip
"Take away the dross from the silver, and there shall come forth a vessel for the finer" (Prov. 25:4).

A Timely Tip
A young school boy was given a plateful of sand. The teacher had told him that there was iron in the sand and it was up to him to try to find it.

First, the young boy shook the dish and strained his eyes to find the iron, but he was unable to see it. Then he took his fingers and ran them through the sand, trying to detect the pieces of iron, but he was still unable to find them.

The instructor said, "There is one easy method, but you still haven't used it." The boy thought for a while, but could not think of an easy method to discover the iron. With a quick motion the teacher took a magnet, drew out the hard-to-find particles of iron from the sand and showed the boy the results.

Sometimes our unthankful hearts are like this boy's straining eyes. We cannot find any good in our daily lives. Sometimes our clumsy fingers get in the way and we cannot see God's blessings and mercies to us. But if, with a thankful heart, like the magnet, we sweep through the day's activities, we will find all of God's blessing to us. They will not only be as iron, but they will be as gold in our lives.

These blessings, like the iron, are mingled with the sand, and we must draw them out each day. We may not see them right away; we may only see the sand. But we can be confident that His blessings are in all things.

Certainly there are blessings in your life. Don't let the few disappointments and discouragements cover up these blessings. Use the magnet of faith and thankfulness, and be happy in God's blessings.

A Final Tip

Blessings hidden or disguised
When revealed are highly prized.

46

BILL D. KARAKTER
(Build a character)

A Bible Tip
Daniel 3:8-18

A Memory Tip

"For the Lord seeth not as man seeth; for man looketh
on the outward appearance, but the Lord looketh on
the heart" (I. Sam. 16:7).

A Timely Tip

It seems that more people today are interested in their
reputations than in their character or convictions.

It has been said that a reputation is what people
think you are, but character is what God knows you
to be.

When you face a really tough situation, and you are
called upon to make a decision, it is then that your
true character shows up. The real you comes through.
You may have the world fooled until a crisis comes
— but then you show what you are really made of.

Shadrach, Meshach, and Abednego showed their true

colors when the crisis came. No doubt, there were lots of people in the camp who were thought to be children of God, but it wasn't until the fiery tests came that these three men stood out, and their true character showed up. Their love for God came first, and God's supreme love for them showed up even in the fiery furnace.

Other people who were merely standing around the furnace, died because of the intense heat! But Shadrach, Meshach, and Abednego were untouched, even though they were right in the flames.

What was their secret? God was with them. Sometime or other, someplace or other, these young Jewish boys had dedicated themselves wholly to the God of Israel — they belonged to Him. They knew that no matter what took place, they could stand true in the power and strength of their God.

What are the fellows and girls saying about you, and what would they say if they knew the real you? What would be your reaction in a time of severe testing? Would you come through as a real Christian, or would you back down and refuse to stand up for the One Who died for you?

A Final Tip

You aren't what folks think you are?
God can bring you up to par.

47

MISS A. LIFLINE
(Miss a lifeline)

A Bible Tip

John 1:1-14

A Memory Tip

"Neither is there salvation in any other: for there is none other name under heaven given among men, whereby we must be saved" (Acts 4:12).

A Timely Tip

A man entered a dark and winding cave one day. He had been warned that it was very dangerous, so he took with him a lamp and a ball of twine. This was done as a precautionary measure to help keep him from getting lost.

Before he entered the cave, he took the ball of twine and tied it to a projection at the entrance. Holding the lamp in one hand and the ball of twine in the other, he then went in.

As he continued to walk farther into the cave, it became darker and darker. How glad he was that he had taken a lamp. Soon he came to a large apartment-like area, and for a short moment he set down his ball of twine and his lamp in order to break off a piece of rock to take back as a souvenir.

Suddenly his lamp fell over and the light went out. Impulsively, the man reached for his ball of twine only to find that his foot had kicked it away while he was reaching for the souvenir. He searched and searched, but all his agonizing efforts to find the ball of twine were in vain.

Many months later his lifeless body was found in the dark cave. He had been careless with regard to the most important thing — the lifeline.

God has provided for us a lifeline — the blood of Jesus Christ. It can be seen all the way through the Bible, from Genesis to Revelation. And yet some people will read the Bible as a book, attend church as a habit, and still refuse to take hold of the "lifeline" that will protect them and spare their lives from eternal judgment.

God has made provision so that we need not perish, but rather have everlasting life. Have you accepted God's lifeline?

A Final Tip

God provides for everyone
Lifeline service, through His Son.

48

JUDGE A. CASE
(Judge a case)

A Bible Tip
Romans 2:1-11

A Memory Tip

"Judge not, and ye shall not be judged: condemn not, and ye shall not be condemned: forgive, and ye shall be forgiven" (Luke 6:37).

A Timely Tip

Judge A. Case had been one of the oustanding judges in the county. When it came to a trial, he sat back quietly, listened to both sides and then counseled the jury. People from all over the country remarked about the fair, honest work of Judge Case. His reputation was good every place — that is, every place but in church. There Judge Case seemed to take upon himself the job of judging.

If someone had to drop out of the choir, the Judge would blurt out, "No doubt he is losing interest." If the pastor preached a sermon in which the Judge was not particularly interested, he would say, "I don't know what is happening to our minister." If the organist played a song Judge Case didn't know too well, he would say, "I don't know why he can't stick to the good old hymns." And if an old song was used in the congregational singing, he would say, "I can't understand why we can't learn some new songs.

Some people seem to find fault with everything. They harshly criticize and condemn others when they should be looking at their own lives. The Bible says, "Judge not, that ye be not judged." Many people judge the motives of their minister, their Sunday school teacher, the choir, their musicians, the people in the pews and everyone, except themselves.

Some people have a habit of coming home from Sunday morning service and making the dinner table a judgment hall.

Rather than judging people, criticizing them and generally pulling them apart, we need to pause for prayer, asking God to work out His will in both their lives and ours.

A Final Tip

The Bible says you should not judge
Or criticize or hold a grudge.

49

WANDA B. POPULAR
(Want to be popular)

A Bible Tip
Titus 2:11-14

A Memory Tip
"For they loved the praise of men more than the praise of God" (John 12:43).

A Timely Tip
Christian fellows and girls are being brought up in an age when popularity and success seem to be life's goal.

I heard a minister say the other day, "Christians have replaced obedience and faithfulness with popularity and success."

I heard a Christian high school girl say a short time ago. "I only have one ambition in life, and that is to be chosen the most popular girl in school.",

I heard a businessman talking to a fellow businessman and say, "All I want is to be a success."

This thinking affects you. More than anything, you want to be a buddy of the most popular fellow in school, or a friend of the most popular girl. You determine that what she does, you will do; where he goes, you will go. The sports he's interested in, you will become interested in.

Most fellows and girls pick an ideal — someone they want to be like, but you need to be careful in picking the right kind of model. Popularity alone may not always be the best way. It may lead to sin.

A Christian teen-ager said recently, "It can't be too wrong if she does it; she's the most popular girl in school."

Are your standards being set according to the standards of some popular girl or fellow? Or are they being made according to God's standards for His people?

How God's heart must ache when He sees His own children following after worldly people and worldly things when He has set up such a beautiful standard for us to follow.

And a final caution — remember the Word says, "Whatsoever a man soweth that shall he also reap."

A Final Tip

Popularity or fad
Sometimes good, but ofttimes bad.

50

MAY KNODENT
(Make no dent)

A Bible Tip

Acts 20:17-24

A Memory Tip

"He that is faithful in that which is least is faithful also in much: and he that is unjust in the least is unjust also in much" (Luke 16:10).

A Timely Tip

When God calls us to do a job, He does not ask us to produce results, He only asks us to be faithful.

Many years ago a minister was greatly discouraged in his work at the church, and thought seriously of leaving it. It seemed so long since any souls had been saved, or since there had been any evidence of real spiritual growth in the lives of his church members.

One night he had a dream. In it he was given a pick and told to go to work on a certain rock. The minister dreamed that he worked hour after hour, and when he looked at the rock, it was hardly dented. Finally, he

106

put down his pick and said to himself, "It is useless. I am getting nowhere."

At that time a stranger came up to him and said, "Are you giving up?"

"Yes," said the minister.

"But, weren't you sent to do this job?" asked the stranger.

"Yes," agreed the minister.

"Then why are you ready to abandon it?"

The minister looked up at the stranger and said, "Look, I have made little or no impression on the rock. My work is in vain."

To this the stranger answered, "What difference does that make? Your job was just to pick. It is not your responsibility if the rock does not yield. The result is not yours."

When the minister awoke, he knew he would continue his duty to preach the Gospel, to teach his people, and God would take care of the results.

Sometimes we get very discouraged when we cannot see results in our work. Perhaps you have witnessed to fellows and girls at school and you have seen no change. God does not ask you to make the change; He merely asks you to be faithful.

A Final Tip

When you feel it doesn't pay,
That's the time to pause and pray.

51

SKIP A. SURVIS
(Skip a service)

A Bible Tip

Psalm 51:6-17

A Memory Tip

"This people draweth nigh unto me with their mouth, and honoureth me with their lips; but their heart is far from me" (Matt. 15:8).

A Timely Tip

Have you ever been bored with church? If you have, you have hardly dared tell your parents or anyone else about it for fear they would think you were backsliding. So you try to cover up and pretend that you enjoyed it. You attended all the services on Sunday, and even went to prayer meeting on a week night. You joined the youth group, but deep inside you were bored to death; and if you would have dared, you would have skipped.

Well, let's face it. If you wouldn't dare tell anyone this, because they might think you were backsliding — are you? If you no longer have the desire to be with

God's people and fellowship with them, if you no longer have the desire to read His Word and spent time in prayer, if you no longer thrill at the old hymns and the Gospel songs that are sung in church, if the choir no longer seems to have a message for you, if the pastor just says words and it seems to go in one ear and out the other — let's face it — maybe you are a backslider.

You have probably thought of a backslider as someone who went into worldly things, but where does it start? Does it start with a lie, when your lips read, "I was glad when they said unto me, let us go into the house of the Lord," but your heart says, "I wish I could get out of here?" Does it start with a lie when your voice sang, "Take my life and let it be consecrated, Lord, to thee," but all the time you are saying, "Lord, I want my own will — I want to do things my way"?

Be honest with yourself, your friends, the people in the church and by all means, with God. What kind of a Christian life are you living? One of pretense? If so, ask God to forgive you, and put a new desire for spiritual things in your heart and life.

A Final Tip
If your heart is filled with guile,
It is time to change your style.

52

I. M. POWTING
(I am pouting)

A Bible Tip

I Peter 5:8-11

A Memory Tip

"Brethren, be not children in understanding: howbeit in malice be ye children, but in understanding be men" (I. Cor. 14:20).

A Timely Tip

Have you ever seen a young child when a toy was taken away from him? In a state of anger he picks up all his other toys and throws them into the trash can. Now, the toys are good, many of them are new, and they certainly do not belong in the trash can. But in a rage or fit of anger, he thinks he does not care if he never sees those toys again. No doubt, there will come a time when he will wish he had not thrown them away. But at the moment, that is not his thought.

I wonder, do we act that way when God does not give us everything we beg for? Sometimes we ask for items that God knows are not best for us to have. Then when we don't get them, we go into a rage and say, "Okay. That's the end; I'm never going to church again; I'll never do this; I'll never do that — it's all over between God and me."

In I Kings 21, a story is recorded about a king who was very pouty.

King Ahab wanted to get his hands on a vineyard that belonged to Naboth, because it was near the king's house. But when he asked Naboth about it, Naboth refused. He tried to explain to the king that it was an inheritance that he had received from his family, and that it wouldn't be right to sell or trade it. If he did such a thing he would disobey God.

But did the king understand? No, he behaved like a little child about the whole matter. He went to his room, threw himself on the bed, turned away his face, and refused to eat. Now that was a real kingly way to act, wasn't it?

How displeased God must be with some of our childish actions. We have years to our credit as far as our age goes, but our actions are so often infantile. Let us determine, by the grace of God, to be adults — mature in His life.

A Final Tip

Baby Christians, there's no doubt,
Often fuss and fume and pout.

53

IMA TASHUN
(Imitation)

A Bible Tip

Acts 8:9-25

A Memory Tip

"Even so ye also outwardly appear righteous unto men, but within ye are full of hypocrisy and iniquity" (Matt. 23:28).

A Timely Tip

Some people think that if they do everything a Christian does, they will automatically become Christians. The Christian goes to church, so the unsaved person begins to attend church. The Christian reads his Bible, so the unsaved person starts to read his Bible. The Christian gives a liberal offering, so the non-Christian gives an offering — however, not often is it very liberal.

Both of them may be doing exactly the same things outwardly, but does that mean their hearts are the same?

When Israel left the land of Egypt, the Egyptians

tried to follow them. They did many things the Israelites did. Pharaoh's magicians had even been able to duplicate some of the miracle plagues that God put upon the land of Egypt, but exercising these powers did not make them God's people.

When He finally led His children out of the land, God miraculously opened a path in the Red Sea, and the Israelites walked through it safely. The Egyptians, overconfident because of their former successes, followed in the steps of the Israelites, only to be destroyed.

God led the children of Israel through the Red Sea, leaving the way open only long enough for the last Israelite to walk through, then He closed it when the Egyptians tried to follow. Israel was safe. The Egyptian army was drowned.

If we do not have genuine Christianity, doom will finally catch up with us. Church going, offering giving, hymn singing, or Bible reading will not save. These things are done by the Christian because he is a Christian, not in order to become a Christian.

A Final Tip
If you're only "playing" church,
Better give God's Word a search.

54

R. U. GRUMBLING
(Are you grumbling)

A Bible Tip
Psalm 147:1-12

A Memory Tip
"Speaking to yourselves in psalms and hymns and spiritual songs, singing and making melody in your heart to the Lord; Giving thanks always for all things unto God and the Father in the name of our Lord Jesus Christ" (Eph. 5:19,20).

A Timely Tip
A group of people had met together for prayer and testimony. At the time the requests were to be given, one man stood to his feet and complained vigorously about his many difficulties. He spoke of his trials on the way to Heaven, and told how glad he would be when God took him away so that all these things would be over.

After he sat down another man stood up and said, "I see our dear brother still lives on Grumble Street.

I used to live there myself. While I was there, I did not enjoy good health, the air was bad, the house was bad, the water was bad, the birds never came and sang on my street. I was gloomy and sad all the time.

"One day I found a vacancy on Thanksgiving Avenue. I moved there, and ever since that time I have been in good health, and so has my family. The air and the water are pure. My house is good. The sun shines on it all day, and the birds keep singing. I too am on my way to heaven, but I'm rejoicing every day."

What an extreme difference in these two men — both Christians, but only one of them was enjoying a victorious Christian life.

Sometimes we find ourselves on Grumble Street, don't we? Everything is wrong; people, places, things; everything. But as quick as we can snap our fingers, we could move to Thanksgiving Avenue. Let's turn our lives completely over to the Lord Jesus and take from Him what He gives us for each day.

Let's vacate from Grumble Street; there's an opening on Thanksgiving Avenue.

A Final Tip

If you live on Grumble Street,
Move to "Thanks" and have a treat.

55

HAL FINDUOUT
(He'll find you out)

A Bible Tip

Romans 5:6-11

A Memory Tip

"If we confess our sins, he is faithful and just to forgive us our sins, and to cleanse us from all unrighteousness" (I John 1:9).

A Timely Tip

The story is told of a man in Siberia who had saved his hard-earned money in a skin purse, which he wore around his waist. Only two other persons, two men, knew about this money.

One day these men decided to murder their friend to get his treasure. After their crime, they began walking toward the forest which was a few miles out of town. As they glanced back, they noticed that they were being followed by two dogs which had been owned by the man whose life they had taken.

The murderers tried many ways to get rid of the

dogs but could not, for they smelled the skin purse. Finally, the criminals decided they would have to kill the dogs, too; but, when they tried, the dogs began to howl dreadfully. After two days of this the two men became so frustrated and frightened that they finally gave themselves up to the authorities, confessing their crime.

The Bible says, "Be sure your sin will find you out." "Whatsoever a man soweth, that shall he also reap." "For the wages of sin is death." "There is none righteous, no not one."

But the Bible also says, "Him that cometh to me I will in no wise cast out." The Bible further says, "Christ died for our sins"; and "Come now, and let us reason together, saith the Lord: though your sins be as scarlet, they shall be as white as snow; though they be red like crimson, they shall be as wool." "The gift of God is eternal life through Jesus Christ our Lord." "For God so loved the world, that he gave His only begotten Son, that whosoever believeth in him should not perish, but have everlasting life."

In Christ there is life; He is the way. All other ways lead to death and destruction.

A Final Tip

Sin will always find you out,
There's no question; there's no doubt.

56

MONTY FROMDAD
(Money from Dad)

A Bible Tip
I Kings 17:8-16

A Memory Tip

"For every beast of the forest is mine, and the cattle upon a thousand hills. I know all the fowls of the mountains: and all the wild beasts of the field are mine. If I were hungry, I would not tell thee: for the world is mine, and the fulness thereof" (Ps. 50:10-12).

A Timely Tip

A young boy was traveling with his father. The boy had no money and no billfold. His father had both. However, when it came time to pay for anything, the young boy simply turned to his father, held out his hand, and received the money. Each time the father would give his son enough money to pay the complete bill.

This was done for the train tickets at the station, for the meals on the diner, for the taxi that took them to their hotel, and for the cost of the hotel room. The young boy had no money of his own, but he was never concerned or worried about it, because he knew his father carried the money. All he needed to do was ask for it, hold out his hand, and receive it.

If you are a Christian, you too are on a journey. You are traveling from earth to Heaven. On this trip you have some definite spiritual needs — needs which you cannot take care of by yourself. So what should you do; worry and fret until all these spiritual needs are automatically cared for? No! Like the little boy, who so completely trusted his father, simply turn to your Father in Heaven. Ask Him to supply, for He has promised; then, by faith hold out your hand and accept His gift. He will always provide.

If it is peace of mind and heart you need, He will supply it. If it is wisdom, He will gladly provide it. If it is strength to overcome temptation He will give it to you.

The little boy's father had never let him down one time, and he was confident that he never would. And it is with such trust that we should approach our heavenly Father. He has never let us down, and He never will.

A Final Tip
He has promised to supply,
And our hearts will satisfy.

57

N. WARD INJURY
(Inward Injury)

A Bible Tip

Matthew 7:15-23

A Memory Tip

"And the Lord said unto him, Now do ye Pharisees make clean the outside of the cup and the platter; but your inward part is full of ravening and wickedness" (Luke 11:39).

A Timely Tip

The accident had just happened, and on the ground lay a man who had been thrown from his car. As people looked at him they agreed that he had not been seriously injured, for there was no outward indication of an injury. Nevertheless, the police officers insisted that the man be taken to the hospital and examined.

Strangely enough, the newspapers reported that evening that the man died about an hour after being admitted to the hospital. He died of internal bleeding.

As the people looked at him, they were sure there

,vas no serious injury, for it didn't show. There hadn't even seemed to be a bruise on his body; nevertheless, the man died!

It might be possible for us to take a drunkard and help him to change his drinking habits, so that he will soon be considered a non-drunkard. Perhaps we could convince the gambler that he should gamble no more. Maybe we could tell the smoking man that he should give up his tobacco. But unless a man has a change inwardly, all of the good efforts will be in vain. For the person who has not accepted Jesus Christ as Saviour is filled with internal sin, and will die a sinner.

The Scriptures say, *"Out of the heart* are the issues of life." A man may change outwardly, but unless his heart is changed, he is still without eternal life. He will die just as surely as the man who died from the internal bleeding, even though nothing could be seen from the outside.

Have you been born again? Have you been washed in the blood of Christ? Or have you merely resolved to be different? If there is no real inward change, you are still doomed to eternal death.

A Final Tip

If your heart is filled with sin,
Face it, you're not genuine.

58

O. N . LEE LAFFTER
(Only laughter)

A Bible Tip
I Corinthians 4:9-16

A Memory Tip
"And they departed from the presence of the council, rejoicing that they were counted worthy to suffer shame for his name. And daily in the temple, and in every house, they ceased not to teach and preach Jesus Christ" (Acts 5:41,42).

A Timely Tip
A man was ridiculed a great deal because of his religious beliefs. He often sacrificed his own possession in order to get an opportunity to witness to someone, and then only to find he was being made fun of. One day someone asked him if he was not ready at times to give up his profession because of all this ridicule.

"No," said the man. "Not after listening to my minister last Sunday."

"Why," said the first man. "What did your minister say?"

"In his sermon he said if we were so foolish to permit people to laugh us out of Christianity until they laughed us into Hell, we had to remember that they could never laugh us out again."

This is serious. Sometimes we are tempted to let the fellows and girls at school laugh us right out of our religious convictions and beliefs. Many young people today do not make a decision for Christ because they are afraid of being ridiculed. Can the laughter of their friends get them out of hell? Never!

Do you suppose the nightingale would really care if a toad despised her singing? There are more important things for us to consider than laughter and ridicule. We must face the real facts.

If we let people laugh us out of putting our trust in the Lord Jesus, we are letting them laugh us right into the Hell that they, too, will share.

Remember, when all is said and done, only those who have trusted Jesus Christ as Saviour and Lord, will be victors.

A Final Tip

When your buddies laugh and scorn
Pity them on judgment's morn.

59

MAY KAY MUMBLE
(Make a mumble)

A Bible Tip
Exodus 4:10-13

A Memory Tip
"My lips shall utter praise, when thou hast taught me thy statutes. My tongue shall speak of thy word: for all thy commandments are righteousness" (Ps. 119:171, 172).

A Timely Tip
"If there is anything I can't stand," said May Mumble's mother, "it is your mumbling something under your breath rather than speaking it clearly."

Have you ever heard that? Some teens have a habit of mumbling. Certainly not you, but other teenagers! They either mumble something under their breath; say it out of the corner of their mouths; whisper it to a friend, or in some other way do not enunciate clearly. And some don't even care to correct this.

We seldom look into the future, so we forget that our speech may be a definite part of our future work for God. The habits we develop today may not be easily broken in later years.

Can't you visualize a "mumbling" preacher, a "garbled-throated" singer or a "corner-mouthed" Sunday school teacher trying to be an effective witness for Christ?

A "hemmer" and a "hawer" is not too impressive in his witness for the Lord Jesus Christ. But God can do wonders with a young person who dedicates even a stuttering, stammering tongue to Him.

Peter was a lowly fisherman, Aaron was only Moses' brother, Amos was a herdsman, and Matthew was a tax gatherer, but God used them all. What your hands find to do, do. Polish anything He has given you, develop it for Him, but be sure to give Him the glory.

Dwight L. Moody preached and Ira D. Sankey sang, and God used them. Billy Graham preaches and Bev Shea sings, and God is using them. But all of them first gave themselves to God.

Learn now to speak clearly and correctly (that goes for pronunciation too) for you are preparing yourself to work for a king — the King of kings.

A Final Tip

When you speak or when you sing,
Do it right; it's for the King.

60

DEWEY YERBEST
(Do your best)

A Bible Tip

Romans 12:1-8

A Memory Tip

"And whatsoever ye do, do it heartily, as to the Lord, and not unto men; Knowing that of the Lord ye shall receive the reward of the inheritance: for ye serve the Lord Christ" (Col. 3:23,24).

A Timely Tip

You may not be a "pro" at everything, but whatever you attempt to do, you should do it to the very best of your ability. No matter what it is — sports, music, school work, church service, or playing, you should determine to do your very best.

Maybe you feel that because you can't do everything Joe Know-It-All does, you are a failure. God didn't ask you to be Joe — He wants you to be you, the best possible you.

God didn't give every Christian the same kind of

talent. Some can sing, others can't carry a tune in a bushel basket. Some can speak, others just stutter or mumble. Some can think on their feet, others have to study, while their hands are running through their hair. Some are born leaders, others flunk out even in the game, "Follow the leader," if they are at the front of the line.

God doesn't expect us to do what the other fellow does. He just wants us to do our very best with what He has given us.

One day the Apostle Peter got a little excited about what John was going to be doing. Peter turned to Jesus and said, "Lord, and what shall this man do?" Jesus had a ready answer for Peter. It was, "What is that to thee, follow thou me" (John 21:22).

Don't be concerned about what the other fellow is going to do. And don't be particularly concerned if you can't do what he is doing. God's Word still says, "What is that to thee, follow thou me." Follow Him with the very best you have. It doesn't matter where, just how. It doesn't matter why, just do.

The talents you have are merely loaned to you by Him. Do the best you can with them. He'll do the rest.

A Final Tip

God will never ask of you
Anything He cannot do.